W9-BYL-737

LAND O LAKES®

AMERICAN HERITAGE
COOKBOOK

TIME-HONORED RECIPES *from* THE FAMILY FARM

CREATIVE
PUBLISHING
international

AMERICAN HERITAGE COOKBOOK

Created by the Editors of Creative Publishing international, Inc.,
in cooperation with Land 'O Lakes, Inc.

Land O'Lakes, Inc.
Arden Hills, Minnesota 55112

Publisher: Pete Theisen
Director, Test Kitchens/Consumer Affairs: Lydia Botham
Editor: Mary Sue Peterson
Coordinating Editor: Cindy Manwarren
Food Editor: Ann L. Burckhardt

For questions regarding recipes in this cookbook of
Land O'Lakes products, please call 1-800-328-4155
or visit us at our Web site at: http://www.landolakes.com

Recipe contributions submitted by
Land O'Lakes Co-op Members and employees and tested
by Land O'Lakes Test Kitchens.

Creative Publishing international, Inc.
5900 Green Oak Drive
Minnetonka, Minnesota 55343

President / CEO: David D. Murphy
Vice President, Custom Services: Sue Riley
Director of Account Management: Jackie Anderson
Executive Food Editor: Carol Frieberg
Art Director: Mark Jacobson
Senior Photographer: Chuck Nields
Photographers: Tate Carlson, Andrea Rugg
Food/Prop Stylists: Abby Wyckoff, Melinda Hutchinson,
  Bobbette Destiche
Project Manager: John Fletcher
Production Manager: Janell Schmidt

Library of Congress Cataloging-in-Publication Data
American heritage cookbook, time-honored recipes from the family farm.
    p.   cm.
  At head of title: Land O'Lakes
  Includes index.
  ISBN 0-86573-172-1 (hc.)
  1. Cookery, American. I. Land O'Lakes, Inc.
TX715.A50815   1999
99-44754   641.5973--dc21   CIP

Printed in the U.S.A. on American paper by: R.R. Donnelley & Sons Co.
10 9 8 7 6 5 4 3 2 1

CONTENTS

The Heritage of Land O'Lakes

A golden reward was offered to the person who could come up with the perfect name. In 1924, the Minnesota Cooperative Creameries Association had been marketing outstanding dairy products for three years, and now needed a brand name that would stand out in the minds of homemakers and indicate the pride and quality that went into their products. Inspired by the warm yellow hue of their butter, the Association offered $200 in gold as first prize in the contest. Out of 100,000 entries,

Ida Foss and George Swift each received the golden prize for separately submitting the winning name: Land O'Lakes.

Since that day, Land O'Lakes has been a leader in providing the freshest and most delicious dairy products nationwide. Land O'Lakes processes 12 billion pounds of milk annually and markets more than 600 dairy products across the United States and throughout the world. Today, Land O'Lakes is the nation's number-one retail butter marketer.

In addition, Land O'Lakes has been outstanding in the field of agricultural research and development. Land O'Lakes provides over 1100 member cooperatives with production materials including feed, seed, plant food and crop protection products, as well as new techniques to increase production and ensure superior quality.

Land O'Lakes remains only as strong as the communities in which its members and employees live and work. It's these people who make Land O'Lakes a thriving food and agricultural company. And it's these people who are honored in the pages of this book. Contributions to this cookbook were received by co-op members throughout the county, and recipes were evaluated by the Land O'Lakes Test Kitchens. Each recipe not only celebrates a slice of American farm life, but also reinforces the commitment from Land O'Lakes to provide wholesome quality ingredients that serve to inspire the creation of winning recipes.

SNACKS & BEVERAGES

*Even small bites taste better
in the company of friends!*

Caramelized Crispy Cereal Snack, page 8
Hot Buttered Cranberry Cider, page 15

CARAMELIZED CRISPY CEREAL SNACK

Prep: 15 min   Microwave: 4 min   Cool: 15 min

2	cups firmly packed brown sugar	1/8	teaspoon salt
1	cup LAND O LAKES® Butter	1/2	teaspoon baking soda
1/2	cup light corn syrup	1	(17.9-ounce) box crunchy corn and rice cereal

1. Combine brown sugar, butter, syrup and salt in 3-quart saucepan. Cook over medium-high heat until mixture comes to a boil (8 to 9 minutes). Continue boiling 1 minute.

2. Remove from heat. Add baking soda; mix well. Pour cereal into large nylon oven roasting bag. Pour syrup over cereal in bag. Shake well to coat.

3. Microwave bag on HIGH, shaking every minute, until well coated (3 to 4 minutes).

4. Spread mixture onto ungreased baking sheet. Cool 15 minutes. Break apart. Store in loosely covered container. *Makes 36 servings (1/2 cup each).*

OVEN DIRECTIONS: Heat oven to 250°. Spray roasting pan with no stick cooking spray. Prepare syrup mixture as directed above. Place cereal in very large bowl. Pour syrup mixture over cereal; toss gently until well coated. Place mixture in prepared roaster. Bake for 40 to 50 minutes, stirring every 15 minutes, or until coating is set. Break apart. Store in loosely covered container.

SUBMITTED BY: DEB WUEBKER, ARCADIA, IA

"This is a perfect recipe to take to a gathering. I don't keep it around the house, because once you start eating it, you don't want to stop!"

CINNAMON TRAIL MIX

Prep: 10 min

4   *cups bite-sized honey and nut crispy rice and corn cereal*

¼   *cup LAND O LAKES® Butter, melted*

2   *teaspoons ground cinnamon*

1   *cup raisins*

1   *cup candy-coated milk chocolate pieces*

1   *(12-ounce) jar dry roasted salted peanuts*

1. Stir together cereal and butter in large bowl. Sprinkle cinnamon evenly over cereal. Add all remaining ingredients; toss lightly. Store in tightly covered container. *Makes 16 servings (½ cup each).*

RECIPE TIP: You may substitute bite-sized crispy wheat squares cereal for the rice and corn cereal.

OPEN-FACE TUNA SANDWICH

Prep: 15 min   Broil: 3 min

1/3   cup mayonnaise

1   (6-ounce) can tuna packed in
      water, drained

2   ounces (1/2 cup) *LAND O LAKES*®
      Cheddar Cheese, shredded

1   *medium (1/2 cup) carrot, shredded*

2   *tablespoons sweet pickle relish*

3   *English muffins, cut in half*

3   *slices LAND O LAKES*® *American*
      Cheese, each cut into 4 strips

1. Heat broiler. Stir together all ingredients **except** muffins and American cheese in small bowl.

2. Place muffins on broiler pan, cut-side up. Broil 4 to 6 inches from heat until muffins are toasted (1 to 2 minutes). Remove from oven. Spread **1/4 cup** tuna mixture on each muffin half; top each with **2 strips** American cheese.

3. Continue broiling until heated through and cheese is melted (2 to 3 minutes). *Makes 6 sandwiches.*

DELI WRAP SNACK

Prep: 15 min

1   (8-inch) homestyle flour tortilla
2   tablespoons garden-style **or** garlic-herb soft cream cheese
3   tablespoons finely shredded carrots
2   tablespoons chopped broccoli florets
1   thin round (³/4-ounce) slice deli cooked ham
1   thin round (³/4-ounce) slice deli cooked turkey breast
1   (1.25-ounce) slice LAND O LAKES® American Cheese
1   (1.25-ounce) slice LAND O LAKES® Mozzarella Cheese

1. Spread tortilla with cream cheese; top with carrots, broccoli, ham, turkey, American cheese and mozzarella cheese. Roll up tightly. Use toothpicks to secure wraps, if desired.

2. To serve, cut in half or cut into 1-inch slices. *Makes 2 servings (¹/2 wrap each).*

SUBMITTED BY: PHYLLIS VANDER POL, SULLY, IA

EASY CHEESE BALLS

Prep: 20 min

2   (8-ounce) packages cream cheese, softened
8   ounces (2 cups) LAND O LAKES® Sharp Cheddar Cheese, shredded
1   tablespoon Worcestershire sauce
1   tablespoon finely chopped onion

1/2   teaspoon cayenne pepper **or** hot pepper sauce
1   cup chopped walnuts **and/or** chopped fresh parsley
    Crackers, celery sticks **and/or** carrot sticks, if desired

1. Beat cream cheese in small mixer bowl on medium speed, scraping bowl often, until smooth. Add all remaining ingredients **except** walnuts, mix well.

2. Divide mixture into two equal portions. Shape each portion into a ball. Roll in walnuts.

3. Serve as a spread with crackers, celery or carrots. *Makes 2 cheese balls (1½ cups each).*

RECIPE TIP: Cheese balls can be made ahead and refrigerated overnight. For an attractive appetizer, roll one in walnuts and one in parsley just before serving.

SUBMITTED BY: MICHELLE ANN SCHUCK, AKRON, OH

"I like this recipe because it's quick and easy, but looks like it took a long time to make!"

BIG HIT CHIVE DIP

Prep: 15 min   Chill: 4 hrs

1/4   cup *LAND O LAKES® Milk*
1   (8-ounce) package cream cheese, softened
1   tablespoon sugar
1/4   cup finely chopped chives
2   tablespoons finely chopped onion
1   tablespoon cider vinegar
      Vegetables, crackers **or** chips

1. Combine milk, cream cheese and sugar in medium mixer bowl. Beat at medium speed, scraping bowl often, until smooth (3 to 4 minutes). Stir in chives, onion and vinegar. Cover; refrigerate to blend flavors (at least 4 hours).

2. Serve with vegetables, crackers or chips. *Makes 1 cup dip.*

SUBMITTED BY: CAROLYN HORST, MIDDLEBURG, PA

LIME CREAM FRUIT DIP

Prep: 10 min   Chill: 30 min

1	cup LAND O LAKES® *Sour Cream*
2	*tablespoons sugar*
1	*tablespoon fresh lime juice*
2	*teaspoons grated lime peel*
	Assorted fresh fruit (apples, cherries, grapes, kiwi fruit, strawberries, etc.)

1. Stir together all ingredients **except** fruit in small bowl. Cover; refrigerate at least 30 minutes.

2. Serve with fresh fruit. *Makes 1 cup dip.*

RECIPE TIP: For a delicious change of pace, substitute orange juice and orange peel for the lime juice and lime peel.

HOT BUTTERED CRANBERRY CIDER

Prep: 10 min   Cook: 16 min

4	cups apple cider **or** apple juice	6	tablespoons *LAND O LAKES*®
4	cups cranberry juice cocktail		Butter, cut-up
1	(3-inch) cinnamon stick	2	tablespoons honey
1	cup light **or** dark rum		Cinnamon sticks, if desired

1. Combine apple cider, cranberry juice cocktail and cinnamon stick in 3-quart saucepan. Cook over medium heat until mixture comes to a boil (8 to 10 minutes). Continue cooking until heated through and flavors are blended (8 to 10 minutes).

2. Remove from heat. Remove cinnamon stick; discard. Add rum, butter and honey; stir until butter melts.

3. To serve, ladle into heated mugs. Garnish with cinnamon stick, if desired. *Makes 8 servings (1 cup each).*

RECIPE TIP: For a festive, non-alcoholic beverage, replace rum with 1 cup apple cider or apple juice.

SPARKLING EGGNOG

Prep: 10 min

4   cups *LAND O LAKES® Half-and-Half*

1   *cup pasteurized refrigerated egg substitute*

1/3   *cup sugar*

1 1/2   *teaspoons ground nutmeg*

2   *teaspoons vanilla*

1   *quart (4 cups) LAND O LAKES® Vanilla Ice Cream, softened*

1   *(28-ounce) bottle lemon-lime carbonated beverage*

1   *cup chopped red **or** green maraschino cherries, if desired*

1. Combine half-and-half, egg substitute, sugar, nutmeg and vanilla in large punch bowl; mix well. Stir in ice cream and carbonated beverage. Garnish with chopped cherries, if desired. *Makes 10 servings (1 cup each).*

RECIPE TIP: Half-and-half, egg substitute, sugar, nutmeg and vanilla can be combined ahead of time and stored, covered, in the refrigerator. Add ice cream and carbonated beverage just before serving.

SUBMITTED BY: SYLVIA KLIMEK, ALEXANDRIA, MN

"We are dairy farmers and, when my eight children and their families are with us on Christmas Eve, no one leaves or goes to bed until the eggnog has been served. This eggnog is part of our family tradition!"

CREAMY ORANGE SIPPER

1 cup *LAND O LAKES*® *Vanilla Ice Cream*

1 cup *orange juice*

1 *(10-ounce) package frozen strawberries in syrup, thawed*

1/2 *teaspoon almond extract*
   Strawberry and orange slices, if desired

1. Place all ingredients in 5–cup blender container. Cover; blend at High speed until smooth (40 to 50 seconds). Garnish with strawberry and orange slices, if desired. Serve immediately. *Makes 3 servings (1 cup each).*

SUBMITTED BY: MARY LOU MCDANIEL, ENGLEVALE, ND

MAIN DISH SUPPERS

Nothing fancy, just hearty home cookin'
stick-to-your-ribs fare!

Casserole From Old Mexico, page 37

OVERNIGHT LASAGNA

Prep: 30 min   Chill: 8 hrs   Bake: 1 hr

2   pounds lean ground beef

1   medium (¹/2 cup) onion, chopped

1¹/2 cups LAND O LAKES® Cottage Cheese

12 ounces (3 cups) LAND O LAKES®
    Mozzarella Cheese, shredded

1   (14.5-ounce) can tomatoes

1   (11.5-ounce) can tomato-vegetable juice

1   (6-ounce) can tomato paste

1   (1.5-ounce) package spaghetti sauce mix

12 (10 x 2¹/4-inch) uncooked dried lasagna noodles

1¹/2 teaspoons anise seed

1. Cook ground beef and onion in 10-inch skillet over medium-high heat, stirring occasionally, until browned (8 to 10 minutes). Drain off fat.

2. Meanwhile, combine cottage cheese and mozzarella cheese in medium bowl. Set aside.

3. Combine tomatoes, tomato-vegetable juice, tomato paste and spaghetti sauce mix in medium bowl; mix well.

4. Spread **¹/2 cup** tomato mixture on bottom of ungreased 13x9-inch baking dish. Top with layer of **4** uncooked lasagna noodles, ¹/3 browned beef, ¹/3 tomato sauce and ¹/3 cheese mixture. Repeat layering twice. Sprinkle with anise seed. Cover; refrigerate 8 hours or overnight.

5. **Heat oven to 375°.** Cover; bake for 45 minutes. Uncover; continue baking for 15 minutes or until bubbly and heated through. Let stand 15 minutes before serving. *Makes 12 servings.*

SUBMITTED BY: KATHLEEN RIGDON, DUNKERTON, IA

"I got this recipe over 15 years ago from a friend. I've made it for my family over the years because it's something they really like and it's easy to make. I think it's the anise seed that makes it taste especially good."

FIESTA BEEF HASH

Prep: 15 min   Cook: 17 min

Hash:

2   pounds ground beef

1   large (³/4 cup) onion, chopped

1   (28-ounce) package frozen O'Brien potatoes

1   teaspoon salt

¹/2 teaspoon pepper

1   (16-ounce) jar salsa

Topping:

8   ounces (2 cups) LAND O LAKES® Colby Cheese, shredded

1   (3.8-ounce) can sliced ripe olives

3   green onions, chopped

1. Cook ground beef and onion in 12-inch skillet or electric frypan over medium-high heat, stirring occasionally, until browned (8 to 10 minutes). Drain off fat.

2. Stir in potatoes, salt and pepper. Cover; continue cooking, stirring occasionally, until potatoes are tender (8 to 10 minutes). Stir in salsa. Continue cooking until heated through (1 to 2 minutes).

3. Sprinkle with cheese; top with olives and green onions. Cover; let stand until cheese is melted (3 to 4 minutes). *Makes 8 servings.*

RECIPE TIP: Leftover chopped cooked potatoes may be substituted for frozen potatoes.

SUBMITTED BY: KARLA PAZOUR, PUKWANA, SD

"My three children helped me prepare this recipe on our local television station in Sioux Falls several years ago. It's a quick and easy skillet supper adapted from a recipe from the Beef Council."

BEEF STROGANOFF

Prep: 50 min   Marinate: 2 hrs   Cook: 45 min

2   tablespoons all-purpose flour

1/2   teaspoon garlic powder

1 1/2 pounds beef sirloin steak, cut into 1/4-inch strips

2   cups dry red wine

3   tablespoons LAND O LAKES® Butter

1   cup (4 ounces) sliced fresh mushrooms

1   teaspoon finely chopped fresh garlic

1   (10 3/4-ounce) can condensed cream of mushroom soup

2   tablespoons ketchup

1/4   teaspoon pepper

12   ounces uncooked dried egg noodles

1   cup LAND O LAKES® Sour Cream

1   tablespoon Worcestershire sauce

1. Place flour and garlic powder in resealable plastic food bag; shake well. Add steak strips; tightly seal bag. Shake bag until steak is well coated. Place beef mixture in shallow glass dish; pour wine over beef. Cover; marinate at least 2 hours or overnight.

2. Remove beef from marinade; **reserve marinade.** Melt butter in 12-inch skillet until sizzling; add beef, mushrooms and garlic. Cook over medium–high heat until mushrooms are tender (5 to 6 minutes). Reduce heat to low; add soup, ketchup and pepper. Cook until beef is fork tender (40 to 45 minutes).

3. Meanwhile, cook egg noodles as directed on package. Drain. Keep warm.

4. Remove skillet from heat. Immediately stir in sour cream and Worcestershire sauce. Serve over hot cooked noodles. *Makes 6 servings.*

RECIPE TIP: If you prefer, the red wine may be replaced with 1 2/3 cups beef broth and 1/3 cup red wine vinegar.

SUBMITTED BY: SUSAN S. HAZEL, WAKEMAN, OH

BIG STONE WALLEYE

Prep: 15 min   Bake: 16 min

1½ pounds fresh walleye fillets

8   thin slices red onion

1   teaspoon seasoned salt

½   teaspoon pepper

2   tablespoons LAND O LAKES®
     Butter, melted

8   thin slices lemon

½   cup LAND O LAKES® Buttermilk

1. Heat oven to 400°. Spray 13x9-inch glass baking dish with no stick cooking spray.

2. Place fillets in single layer in prepared pan; cover with onion. Sprinkle with seasoned salt and pepper; drizzle with butter. Top with lemon. Pour buttermilk around fillets.

3. Cover; bake for 16 to 20 minutes or until fish flakes with a fork. Garnish with fresh dill sprigs if desired. *Makes 6 servings.*

RECIPE TIP: If you don't have buttermilk, substitute 1½ teaspoons vinegar plus enough milk to equal ½ cup.

SUBMITTED BY: DENNIS KASSUBE,
BIG STONE CITY, SD

POPOVER PIZZA

Prep: 30 min   Bake: 25 min

Filling:

1	*pound ground beef* **or** *pork sausage*
1	*cup chopped red pepper*
1	*large (1 cup) onion, chopped*
1/2	*cup sliced fresh mushrooms*
1	*(28-ounce) jar thick-style spaghetti sauce*
1	*(2.25-ounce) can sliced ripe olives, drained*
8	*ounces (2 cups) LAND O LAKES® Mozzarella Cheese, shredded*

Topping:

2	*eggs, room temperature*
1	*cup LAND O LAKES® Milk, room temperature*
1	*tablespoon vegetable oil*
1	*cup all-purpose flour*
1/2	*teaspoon salt*
1/2	*cup grated Parmesan cheese*

1. Heat oven to 400°. Combine ground beef, red pepper and onion in 10-inch skillet. Cook over medium-high heat, stirring occasionally, until onion is softened and beef is browned (6 to 8 minutes). Drain off fat. Stir in mushrooms, spaghetti sauce and olives. Spoon into ungreased 13x9-inch baking pan. Top with mozzarella cheese. Place baking pan in oven to heat while preparing topping.

2. Beat eggs in small mixer bowl at medium speed, scraping bowl often, until light and lemon-colored (1 to 2 minutes). Add milk and oil; continue beating 1 minute. Stir in flour and salt, with wire whisk until smooth. Pour mixture over hot filling, spreading to cover filling completely. Sprinkle with Parmesan cheese.

3. Bake for 25 to 30 minutes or until top is puffed and golden brown. DO NOT OPEN OVEN DOOR DURING BAKING. Serve immediately. *Makes 12 servings.*

RECIPE TIP: If you prefer, you may substitute 8 ounces of sliced pepperoni for the ground beef. Just add it (uncooked) with the mushrooms, spaghetti sauce and olives.

"I am a single father raising two sons, ages 10 and 11. My boys love this quick and easy recipe. When we're having it for supper, they like to invite their friends over."

HERB—MARINATED PORK TENDERLOIN

Prep: 15 min   Marinate: 3 hrs   Grill: 40 min

- 1/2 cup white wine **or** chicken broth
- 1/4 cup olive **or** vegetable oil
- 1/4 cup chopped fresh rosemary **or**
  1 tablespoon dried rosemary
- 2 tablespoons chopped fresh sage leaves
  or 2 teaspoons dried sage leaves
- 2 tablespoons chopped fresh thyme leaves
  or 2 teaspoons dried thyme leaves
- 2 teaspoons finely chopped fresh garlic
- 2 pounds pork tenderloin

1. Combine all ingredients **except** pork in large resealable plastic food bag; add pork tenderloin. Tightly seal bag. Turn bag several times to coat pork well. Place in 13x9-inch pan. Refrigerate, turning occasionally, at least 3 hours or overnight.

2. **Prepare grill;** heat until coals are ash white. Remove pork from marinade; **reserve marinade.**

3. Place pork on grill. Cover; grill, turning and basting occasionally with marinade, until meat thermometer reaches 160°F (Medium) or desired doneness (40 to 50 minutes). *Makes 8 servings.*

SAUSAGE & CHEESE BISCUIT BAKE

Prep: 40 min   Bake: 10 min

Dough:

3   cups all-purpose flour

1   tablespoon baking powder

1   teaspoon salt

1/2   cup cold LAND O LAKES® Butter

1   cup LAND O LAKES® Milk

Topping:

1   pound pork sausage, browned, drained

8   (3/4-ounce each) LAND O LAKES®
     American Cheese Slices

     Thick and chunky salsa, if desired

     LAND O LAKES® Sour Cream, if desired

1. Heat oven to 450°. Combine flour, baking powder and salt in large bowl; cut in butter until crumbly. Stir in milk just until moistened. Divide dough in half.

2. Roll out **half** of dough to 13x9-inch rectangle. Place dough in bottom of greased 13x9-inch baking pan. Sprinkle cooked sausage over dough; top evenly with cheese. Roll out remaining dough to 13x9-inch rectangle; cut into 12 (3x3-inch) squares. Arrange biscuit squares over cheese. Bake for 10 to 12 minutes or until lightly browned.

3. To serve, cut into 12 servings. Top each serving with salsa and sour cream, if desired. *Makes 12 servings.*

SUBMITTED BY: JUANNA BETH LEWIS, MILBURN, NE

"My husband and I farm and ranch 8,000 acres in the Nebraska Sandhills with our seven children. We like quick and easy dishes for Sunday evening suppers. This recipe is perfect with a salad or vegetable to complete the meal."

SUBMITTED BY: JANA KASTER, HULL, IA

*"My husband vowed never to eat spinach
until he tasted this dish."*

30
MAIN DISH SUPPERS

SPINACH-CHICKEN ENCHILADA CASSEROLE

Prep: 45 min   Bake: 30 min

2   tablespoons *LAND O LAKES® Butter*

¹/₄   cup chopped onion

4   boneless skinless chicken breasts, cut into thin strips

1   cup *LAND O LAKES® Sour Cream*

³/₄   cup *LAND O LAKES® Milk*

1   (10³/₄-ounce) can condensed cream of mushroom soup

1   (10-ounce) package frozen chopped spinach, thawed, well-drained

1   teaspoon garlic powder

1   teaspoon onion powder

8   ounces (2 cups) *LAND O LAKES® Mozzarella Cheese, shredded*

8   flour tortillas

4   ounces (1 cup) *LAND O LAKES® American Cheese, shredded*

1. Heat oven to 350°. Melt butter in 10-inch skillet until sizzling; add onion and chicken strips. Cook over medium heat, stirring occasionally, until chicken is no longer pink (5 to 7 minutes).

2. Combine sour cream, milk, soup, spinach, garlic powder and onion powder in medium bowl; mix well. Spread **1 cup** sour cream mixture on bottom of greased 13x9-inch baking dish.

3. Place ¹/₈ chicken, **2 tablespoons** mozzarella cheese and **2 tablespoons** American cheese in center of each tortilla; roll up. Repeat with remaining ingredients. Place tortillas in prepared dish, seam-side down.

4. Spread with remaining sour cream mixture. Sprinkle with remaining mozzarella cheese. Bake for 30 to 35 minutes or until bubbly and heated through. *Makes 8 servings.*

CHICKEN PIZZA

Prep: 20 min   Bake: 19 min

1   (10-ounce) package refrigerated pizza dough
1   tablespoon LAND O LAKES® Butter
³/4 pound boneless skinless chicken breast
¹/2 teaspoon dried basil leaves
¹/2 teaspoon garlic powder
¹/2 teaspoon dried oregano leaves
1   (9-ounce) container refrigerated Alfredo pasta sauce

1   cup (4 ounces) sliced fresh mushrooms
1   medium zucchini, thinly sliced
1   small red **or** green pepper, thinly sliced
1   green onion, thinly sliced
6   ounces (1¹/2 cups) LAND O LAKES® Mozzarella Cheese, shredded
¹/4 cup grated Parmesan cheese

1. Heat oven to 425°. Lightly grease 12 or 14-inch pizza pan. Unroll pizza dough; press into prepared pan. Prick dough with fork. Bake for 7 to 10 minutes or until browned and crisp.

2. Meanwhile, melt butter in 10-inch skillet until sizzling; add chicken, basil, garlic powder and oregano. Cook over medium heat until chicken is no longer pink (5 to 7 minutes). Remove chicken from skillet. Cut into strips.

3. Spread pasta sauce over partially baked crust. Arrange cooked chicken strips on sauce; top with mushrooms, zucchini, green pepper and green onion. Sprinkle with mozzarella and Parmesan cheese.

4. Bake for 12 to 14 minutes or until cheese is melted and vegetables are heated through. *Makes 6 servings.*

SUBMITTED BY: CHERYL FLYNN, NORTH SIOUX CITY, SD

*"My kids could eat pizza 7 days a week
—and they love my chicken pizza."*

MAIN DISH SUPPERS

CHICKEN WITH TINY BISCUITS

Prep: 20 min   Bake: 1 hr

Filling:

2   cups cooked chicken, cut-up

1½ cups (8 ounces) frozen cut green beans **or** peas

½   cup water

1   (10¾-ounce) can condensed cream of chicken
    soup

½   teaspoon ground sage

Biscuits:

1   cup all-purpose flour

1¼ teaspoons baking powder

¼   teaspoon salt

⅛   teaspoon baking soda

3   tablespoons cold LAND O LAKES® Butter

½   cup LAND O LAKES® Buttermilk

1. Heat oven to 375°. Combine all filling ingredients in ungreased 2-quart casserole. Set aside.

2. Combine flour, baking powder, salt and baking soda in medium bowl; cut in butter until crumbly. Stir in buttermilk just until moistened. Turn dough onto lightly floured surface; knead until smooth (1 minute).

3. Roll out dough to 1-inch thick circle. Cut into biscuits with 1-inch floured biscuit cutter.

4. Place biscuits on top of chicken mixture. Cover; bake for 45 minutes. Uncover; continue baking for 15 to 20 minutes or until biscuits are golden brown and filling is bubbly. Garnish with fresh sage leaves, if desired. *Makes 4 servings*

RECIPE TIP: If you don't have buttermilk, substitute 1½ teaspoons vinegar plus enough milk to equal ½ cup.

SUBMITTED BY: MARY HERNESS, WHITEHALL, WI

"Our family is traditionally a meat, potatoes and vegetable family. I have been searching for a hot dish recipe that would be quick and acceptable to them—this one passed the test!"

PAN-ROASTED TURKEY & VEGETABLES

Prep: 15 min   Bake: 40 min

Turkey:

1/4	cup LAND O LAKES® Butter
1/2	teaspoon dried thyme leaves
1/4	teaspoon salt
1/4	teaspoon coarsely ground pepper
2	(3/4 pound each) turkey tenderloins

Vegetables:

3	cups cauliflower florets (1 pound)
2	cups broccoli florets (5 ounces)
4	medium carrots, sliced
2	small onions, cut into quarters

1. Heat oven to 400°. Melt butter in oven-safe Dutch oven or small roasting pan until sizzling; stir in thyme, salt and pepper. Add turkey tenderloins. Cook over medium-high heat, turning occasionally, until browned on all sides (8 to 10 minutes).

2. Add cauliflower, broccoli, carrots and onions to turkey. Cover; bake for 40 to 45 minutes or until turkey is no longer pink and vegetables are crisply tender. Serve with pan juices. *Makes 6 servings.*

CASSEROLE
FROM OLD MEXICO

Prep: 15 min   Bake: 20 min

1 cup all-purpose baking mix	1 (4-ounce) can whole green chilies, drained
½ cup LAND O LAKES® Milk	8 ounces (2 cups) LAND O LAKES®
1 (15-ounce) can whole kernel corn, drained	Monterey Jack **or** Cheddar Cheese, sliced
1 egg, beaten	Salsa, if desired
2 tablespoons LAND O LAKES® Butter, melted	LAND O LAKES® Sour Cream, if desired

1. Heat oven to 400°. Combine baking mix, milk, corn, egg and melted butter in medium bowl; mix well. Spread **half** of batter in well-greased 8-inch square baking dish.

2. Cut chilies in half to lay flat. Place chilies over batter; top with cheese. Spread remaining batter over cheese. Bake for 20 to 22 minutes or until golden brown.

3. To serve, cut into squares. Top each serving with salsa and sour cream, if desired. *Makes 9 servings.*

SUBMITTED BY: SILAS K. GILLIAM, HERMISTON, OR

"My four brothers and I grew up on a ranch in Northern Arizona. We lived so far from town that my mom and dad only made a trip to Phoenix for supplies once a month. Before leaving, we made sure Mom had on her list all the ingredients needed for this dish."

VEGETABLE MACARONI & CHEESE

Prep: 45 min   Bake: 40 min

2 cups (7 to 8 ounces) uncooked dried elbow macaroni

1 cup LAND O LAKES® Milk

8 ounces (2 cups) LAND O LAKES® American Cheese, shredded

3 eggs, slightly beaten

1 teaspoon salt

1/4 teaspoon pepper

1/2 cup shredded carrots

1/4 cup finely chopped green pepper

1/4 cup finely chopped onion

1 (14.5-ounce) can stewed tomatoes, drained

1 cup fresh bread cubes

2 tablespoons LAND O LAKES® Butter, melted

1. Cook macaroni according to package directions. Drain.

2. Heat oven to 350°. Combine cooked macaroni, milk, cheese, eggs, salt and pepper in large bowl; mix well. Stir in carrots, green pepper, onion and tomatoes. Spoon into ungreased 2-quart casserole.

3. Combine bread cubes and melted butter in small bowl; toss lightly. Sprinkle cubes evenly over casserole. Bake for 40 to 45 minutes or until thoroughly heated and bubbly. Let stand 10 minutes before serving. *Makes 6 servings.*

SUBMITTED BY: SHIRLEE NELSON, MARCUS, IA

"Growing up on a farm meant a life full of work, but our sons helped with chores, gardens and yard work. It didn't seem like work when you worked together."

VEGGIES, BREADS & SIDES

Garden-fresh greens, vegetables and homemade breads—
foods that play a supporting role.

Creamy Herb Dressing with Mixed Greens, page 56
Everyone's Favorite Buns, page 57

BAKED CARROT CASSEROLE

Prep: 30 min   Bake: 35 min

Carrots:

6 to 8 medium (4 cups) carrots, sliced 1/4-inch

2   tablespoons *LAND O LAKES® Butter*

1/4   cup finely chopped celery

2   tablespoons all-purpose flour

1/2   teaspoon salt

1/4   teaspoon dry mustard

1   cup *LAND O LAKES® Milk*

4   ounces (1 cup) *LAND O LAKES®
     American Cheese,* cubed

Topping:

2 to 3 slices (1 1/2 cups) fresh bread, cubed
     1/2-inch

2   tablespoons *LAND O LAKES® Butter,* melted

1. Place carrots in 2-quart saucepan; add enough water to cover. Cook over medium heat until just tender (8 to 10 minutes). Drain. Place cooked carrots in 8-inch square baking dish.

2. Heat oven to 350°. Melt 2 tablespoons butter until sizzling in 2-quart saucepan until sizzling; add celery. Cook over medium heat, stirring occasionally, until crisply tender (3 to 4 minutes).

3. Stir in flour, salt and dry mustard. Continue cooking, stirring occasionally, until bubbly (1 minute). Stir in milk with wire whisk. Continue cooking, stirring occasionally, until mixture thickens and comes to a full boil (4 to 5 minutes). Continue boiling 1 minute. Remove from heat; stir in cheese until melted.

4. Pour sauce over carrots. Stir together bread cubes and 2 tablespoons butter in small bowl. Sprinkle over carrots. Bake for 35 to 40 minutes or until bubbly in center and bread cubes are lightly browned. *Makes 8 servings (1/2 cup each) .*

MASHED POTATO CASSEROLE

Prep: 30 min   Bake: 55 min

4   large (2½ to 3 pounds) potatoes, peeled, cut into eighths

¼   cup *LAND O LAKES® Milk*

½   teaspoon salt

1   cup *LAND O LAKES® Sour Cream*

1   cup *LAND O LAKES® Cottage Cheese*

¼   cup finely chopped onion

1   egg, beaten

½   cup (14) crushed saltine crackers

2   tablespoons *LAND O LAKES® Butter, melted*

1. Place potatoes in 2-quart saucepan. Add enough water to cover. Cook over high heat until water comes to a boil. Reduce heat to medium. Cook until potatoes are fork tender (15 to 18 minutes). Drain.

2. **Heat oven to 325°.** Place potatoes in large bowl. Add milk and salt. Mash potatoes with potato masher until smooth. Stir in sour cream, cottage cheese, onion and egg; mix well.

3. Spoon potato mixture into ungreased 2-quart casserole. Combine cracker crumbs and melted butter in small bowl; sprinkle evenly over potatoes. Bake for 55 to 65 minutes or until throughly heated through and topping is golden. *Makes 8 servings (¾ cup each) .*

SUBMITTED BY: BEVERLY JANSEN, TURTLE LAKE, WI

*"This recipe was given to me by a friend who is known to be a great cook!
It's become a family favorite. I also make it for large gatherings
where people frequently ask me for the recipe."*

SWEET 'N CREAMY CORN

Prep: 10 min   Cook: 2 hrs

2   (16-ounce) bags frozen whole kernel corn
1   (8-ounce) package regular **or** light cream cheese, cubed
1/4   cup LAND O LAKES® Butter, cut-up
2   tablespoons sugar

1. Combine all ingredients in electric slow cooker. Cook on High for 2 to 2½ hours, or on Low for 4 to 5 hours, stirring once or twice, or until flavors are well blended. *Makes 12 servings (½ cup each).*

RECIPE TIP: Leftover corn reheats well in the microwave oven.

SUBMITTED BY: ANNETTE WINRICK, FORT DODGE, IA

"Church suppers were a highlight growing up in rural Kansas— this dish was always a favorite. I submit this recipe in honor of all the wonderful cooks at Fowler United Methodist Church. It's still a favorite at our family gatherings, today."

WILD RICE CASSEROLE

Prep: 40 min   Bake: 45 min

4   cups water

1   cup uncooked wild rice

1   teaspoon salt

¼   cup LAND O LAKES® Butter

1   cup chopped carrots

1   cup sliced celery

1   cup chopped onions

1   (6-ounce) can mushroom stems and
    pieces, drained

1   teaspoon poultry seasoning, if desired

1. Combine water, wild rice and
½ teaspoon salt in 2-quart saucepan.
Cook over medium heat until mixture
comes to a full boil (6 to 8 minutes).
Reduce heat to low. Cover; cook until
rice just begins to split open (30 to 40
minutes). Drain. Stir in butter.

2. **Heat oven to 350°.** Combine
cooked rice mixture, remaining salt,
carrots, celery, onion and mushrooms
in ungreased 2-quart casserole. Bake for
45 to 50 minutes or until heated
through. *Makes 10 servings (½ cup each).*

SUBMITTED BY: EVELYN MEECH, SEBEKA, MN

*"This is a favorite recipe of mine, because it does not call for canned soup
like so many others, and it has a delicious buttery flavor."*

GREEN BEANS WITH RED PEPPER & BACON

Prep: 10 min   Cook: 18 min

5   slices bacon

1   medium (1/2 cup) onion, coarsely
    chopped

1   medium (1/2 cup) red pepper, coarsely
    chopped

2   cups frozen cut green beans

1. Cook bacon in 10-inch skillet over medium heat until crisp (8 to 10 minutes). Remove bacon from pan; **reserve 1 tablespoon pan drippings.** Crumble bacon; set aside.

2. Add onion and red pepper to reserved pan drippings in same skillet. Cook over medium heat, stirring occasionally, until tender (3 to 5 minutes). Stir in beans. Continue cooking until beans are crisply tender (7 to 9 minutes). Stir in bacon. *Makes 4 servings.*

CHEESY-DIJON CAULIFLOWER

Prep: 10 min   Microwave: 10 min

1   medium head (about 2½ pounds)
    cauliflower, broken into florets
2   tablespoons water
½   cup mayonnaise **or** salad dressing
1   teaspoon finely chopped onion
1   teaspoon Dijon-style mustard
2   ounces (½ cup) *LAND O LAKES®*
    Cheddar Cheese, shredded

1. Place cauliflower in ungreased 1½-
quart casserole; add water. Microwave
on HIGH until crisply tender (8 to 9
minutes). Drain.

2. Combine mayonnaise, onion and
mustard in small bowl. Spoon over cauliflower. Sprinkle with cheese. Microwave
on MEDIUM until sauce is heated
through and cheese is melted (1½ to
2 minutes). Let stand 2 minutes before
serving. *Makes 9 servings (½ cup each).*

SUBMITTED BY: MARION ENTINGER, BELLE PLAINE, MN

*"I make this dish often, because all
of my four children enjoy it!"*

SCALLOPED CABBAGE

Prep: 25 min   Cook: 20 min   Bake: 35 min

1 large (3 to 4 pound) head cabbage	$1/8$ teaspoon pepper
$1/2$ cup LAND O LAKES® Butter	3 cups LAND O LAKES® Milk
$1/2$ cup all-purpose flour	$1 1/3$ cups (36) crushed saltine crackers
$1/2$ teaspoon salt	

1. Heat oven to 350°. Wash cabbage; remove core. Cut into quarters; coarsely chop.

2. Place cabbage in Dutch oven. Add enough water to cover cabbage half way. Cover; cook over high heat until mixture comes to a boil (10 to 12 minutes). Uncover; reduce heat to medium. Cook until cabbage is just tender (3 to 4 minutes). DO NOT OVERCOOK. Drain. Set aside.

3. Melt **6 tablespoons** butter in 2-quart saucepan over medium heat; stir in flour, salt and pepper. Cook until smooth and bubbly (1 minute). Stir in milk with wire whisk. Continue cooking, stirring constantly, until mixture thickens and comes to a full boil (4 to 6 minutes). Continue boiling 1 minute.

4. Layer **half** of cabbage, **half** of white sauce, remaining cabbage and remaining white sauce in 3-quart casserole.

5. Melt remaining 2 tablespoons butter in microwave on HIGH in small bowl (30 to 60 seconds). Add cracker crumbs; toss until well coated. Sprinkle over casserole. Bake for 35 to 45 minutes or until heated through. *Makes 12 servings (1 cup each).*

SUBMITTED BY: JUDY HAINES, ANKENY, IA

"My mother traditionally brought this dish to the family reunion potluck each year since 1945. My mother passed away several years ago, but she left us a legacy of wonderful recipes. Now we also serve it at our house for Thanksgiving and Christmas."

CREAMY POTATO SOUP

Prep: 15 min   Cook: 21 min

¼   cup *LAND O LAKES® Butter*

5   *medium (4 cups) potatoes, peeled, cubed*

¼   *cup chopped onion*

2   *teaspoons chicken-flavored bouillon
      granules*

½   *teaspoon salt*

⅛   *teaspoon pepper*

2   *cups LAND O LAKES® Milk
      LAND O LAKES® Cheddar
      Cheese, shredded, if desired*

1. Place all ingredients **except** milk and cheese in 4-quart saucepan. Add enough water to cover. Cook over medium–high heat until mixture comes to a boil (8 to 10 minutes). Continue cooking until potatoes are tender (10 to 12 minutes).

2. Remove from heat. Stir in milk. Pour **half** of soup mixture into blender container. Cover; blend until smooth (25 to 30 seconds). Return to saucepan. Cook over medium heat until heated through (3 to 5 minutes). To serve, spoon into individual soup bowls. Top with cheese and green onions, if desired. *Makes 6 servings (1 cup each).*

SUBMITTED BY: DENISE J. FETZER, MAIDEN ROCK, WI

TEN-DOLLAR POTATOES

Prep: 45 min   Chill: 4 hrs   Cook: 1 hr

3   *pounds russet potatoes, boiled, peeled, cooled*
1/4 *cup LAND O LAKES® Butter*
1   *(10 3/4-ounce) can condensed cream of chicken soup*
2   *cups LAND O LAKES® Sour Cream*

5   *ounces (1 1/4 cups) LAND O LAKES® Cheddar Cheese, shredded*
3   *tablespoons finely chopped onion*
1/2 *teaspoon salt*
1/2 *teaspoon pepper*

1. Shred cooked potatoes into large bowl. Set aside.

2. Melt **2 tablespoons** butter in 2-quart saucepan; add soup. Cook over medium heat, stirring occasionally, until smooth (3 to 5 minutes). Remove from heat. Stir in sour cream, cheese, onion, salt and pepper. Add to potatoes; mix well.

3. Spoon potato mixture into ungreased 13x9-inch baking dish. Melt remaining 2 tablespoons butter; drizzle over potato mixture. Cover; refrigerate 4 hours or overnight.

4. **Heat oven to 350°.** Bake for 60 to 65 minutes or until heated through and golden brown.
Makes 16 servings (1/2 cup each).

RECIPE TIP: To save time, substitute one (32-ounce) bag frozen hash brown potatoes for the shredded russet potatoes. Stir frozen potatoes into sour cream mixture before spooning into baking dish.

SUBMITTED BY: FRANCES B. MUSSER, NEWMANSTOWN, PA

*"I adapted this recipe from one I found in a farm magazine years ago.
I keep it in my file and make it often for potlucks and community suppers.
It goes well with many different foods."*

GARDEN PASTA SALAD

Prep: 40 min   Chill: 12 hrs

Salad:

12 ounces (3 cups) uncooked dried rotini (corkscrew or pasta twists)

2 cups (5 stalks) chopped celery

8 ounces (2 cups) LAND O LAKES® Cheddar Cheese, cubed

2 medium (1 cup) carrots, shredded

1 medium (1/2 cup) green pepper, chopped

Dressing:

1 cup sugar

1/2 cup white vinegar **or** cider vinegar

1/3 cup vegetable oil

Salt

Pepper

Fresh thyme sprigs, if desired

1. Cook rotini according to package directions. Rinse with cold water. Drain.

2. Combine all salad ingredients in large bowl.

3. Stir together sugar, vinegar and oil in small bowl until sugar dissolves. Pour dressing over salad; toss until well-coated. Cover; refrigerate, stirring occasionally, until flavors are blended (12 hours or overnight).

4. Just before serving, add salt and pepper to taste. Garnish with thyme sprigs, if desired.
Makes 24 servings (1/2 cup each).

SUBMITTED BY: CONNIE L. FREDERICK, DENMARK, WI

CALICO CABBAGE SLAW

Prep: 15 min

Dressing:

1 cup mayonnaise **or** salad dressing

2 tablespoons sugar

2 tablespoons cider vinegar

1 tablespoon Dijon-style mustard

$^1/_2$ teaspoon dried dill weed

Salad:

1 (16-ounce) package (8 cups) coleslaw mix

8 ounces (2 cups) *LAND O LAKES®* *Chedarella® Cheese*, cubed $^1/_4$-inch

1 (11-ounce) can whole kernel corn with red and green peppers, well-drained

1 (2.25-ounce) can sliced ripe olives, drained

1. Combine all dressing ingredients in small bowl; mix well.

2. Combine all salad ingredients in large bowl. Pour dressing over salad; toss until well-coated. *Makes 10 servings ($^3/_4$ cup each).*

54
VEGGIES, BREADS & SIDES

PINEAPPLE CHEESE MOLD

Prep: 30 min   Chill: 6 hrs, 45 min

1   (20-ounce) can crushed pineapple, well-drained, **reserve 3/4 cup juice**

3/4   cup sugar

1   (1/4-ounce) envelope unflavored gelatin

1/3   cup water

1   tablespoon lemon juice

2   cups LAND O LAKES® Cottage Cheese

2/3   cup mayonnaise

2/3   cup LAND O LAKES® Whipping Cream, whipped

4   ounces (1 cup) LAND O LAKES® Cheddar Cheese, shredded

    Lettuce

    Pineapple tidbits, LAND O LAKES® Cheddar Cheese, shredded, **or** maraschino cherries, if desired

1. Pour reserved pineapple juice into small saucepan. Add sugar. Cook over medium-high heat, stirring constantly, until mixture comes to a boil (3 to 4 minutes).

2. Meanwhile, soften gelatin in water in small bowl. Add gelatin mixture to hot juice mixture. Reduce heat to low. Cook, stirring occasionally, until gelatin is dissolved (3 to 5 minutes). Remove from heat. Stir in lemon juice. Refrigerate until slightly thickened (45 to 60 minutes).

3. Add drained pineapple, cottage cheese, mayonnaise, whipped cream and cheddar cheese to gelatin mixture; stir well. Spoon into greased 8-inch square baking dish. Refrigerate until firm (6 hours or overnight).

4. To serve, line large platter or individual serving plates with lettuce. Cut gelatin into squares; place on lettuce-lined platter. Garnish with pineapple tidbits, shredded cheese or maraschino cherries, if desired. *Makes 12 servings.*

SUBMITTED BY: VERA HAVLAT, DORCHESTER, NE

"My bachelor brother makes this salad as his contribution to holiday meals. It's full of good dairy products from the farm. We don't milk anymore, but still enjoy lots of milk products."

CREAMY HERB DRESSING WITH MIXED GREENS

Prep: 20 min   Chill: 1 hr

Dressing:

1   cup LAND O LAKES® Sour Cream

1/2   cup finely chopped peeled seeded cucumber

1/4   cup finely chopped red pepper

2 to 3 sprigs fresh parsley, finely chopped

1   tablespoon finely chopped fresh celery leaves

1   tablespoon finely chopped green onion

2   tablespoons LAND O LAKES® Milk

1   teaspoon dried dill weed

1/2   teaspoon salt

Salad:

Mixed salad greens (leaf lettuce, Bibb lettuce, spinach or romaine) **or** 1 (10-ounce) bag fancy mixed salad greens

1. Combine all dressing ingredients in small bowl; mix well. Cover; refrigerate at least 1 hour.

2. To serve, place greens in individual salad bowls. Serve with dressing. *Makes 1½ cups dressing (2 tablespoons per serving).*

EVERYONE'S FAVORITE BUNS

Prep: 30 min   Rise: 1 hr, 45 min   Bake: 14 min

¹/₂	cup LAND O LAKES® Milk	1	egg
6	tablespoons LAND O LAKES® Butter	1	teaspoon salt
	Warm water (105 to 115°)	2	(¹/₄-ounce) packages active dry yeast
¹/₂	cup sugar		5 to 5¹/₂ cups bread flour

1. Place milk and **4 tablespoons** butter in 2-cup glass measuring cup. Microwave on HIGH for 1¹/₂ minutes. Add enough warm water to measure 2 cups.

2. Combine sugar, egg and salt in large mixer bowl; mix well. Add milk mixture; mix well. Stir in yeast; let stand 2 minutes.

3. Add **3 cups** flour. Beat at medium speed, scraping bowl often, until smooth (2 to 3 minutes). Add 2 cups flour. Continue beating until smooth (2 to 3 minutes). Stir in enough remaining flour by hand to make dough easy to handle.

4. Place dough in greased bowl. Melt remaining 2 tablespoons butter; brush top of dough. **Reserve remaining melted butter.** Cover; let dough rise until double in size (about 45 minutes). (Dough is ready if indentation remains when touched.)

5. Punch down dough; divide dough in half. Shape each half on lightly floured surface into 12 buns. Place buns on two greased 15x10x1-inch jelly-roll pans. Brush with reserved melted butter. Cover; let rise until double in size (about 1 hour).

6. **Heat oven to 375°.** Bake for 14 to 16 minutes or until golden brown. Remove from pan immediately. Brush buns with reserved melted butter, if desired. *Makes 24 buns.*

SUBMITTED BY: SHARON NELSON, PRAIRIE FARM, WI

"I am the designated bun maker in our family! I get lots of practice making these buns for occasions such as graduations, Christmas and Easter."

JO'S PIZZA ROLLS

Prep: 1 hr, 10 min   Rise: 1 hr, 30 min   Bake: 20 min

Dough:

3¹/4 to 3³/4 cups all-purpose flour	2 tablespoons LAND O LAKES® Butter	1 ounce (¹/4 cup) LAND O LAKES® Mozzarella Cheese, shredded
1¹/2 teaspoons active dry yeast	1¹/2 teaspoons salt	2 ounces (¹/2 cup) LAND O LAKES® Hot Pepper Monterey Jack Cheese, shredded
¹/2 teaspoon garlic powder	1 teaspoon pepper	
¹/2 teaspoon dried oregano leaves	**Filling:**	
1¹/2 cups water	¹/2 cup chopped pepperoni	**Egg Wash:**
¹/4 cup finely chopped onion	4 slices (¹/4 cup) cooked bacon, crumbled	1 egg, beaten
2 tablespoons nonfat dry milk powder	1 (4-ounce) can mushrooms, finely chopped	2 tablespoons water
2 tablespoons sugar		

1. Place **2 cups** flour, yeast, garlic powder and oregano in large mixer bowl. Set aside.

2. Place water, onion, dry milk, sugar, butter, salt and pepper in 1-quart saucepan. Cook over medium heat, stirring occasionally, until mixture reaches 120 to 130° (2 to 4 minutes). Add milk mixture to flour mixture. Beat at low speed, scraping bowl often, until well mixed (1 to 2 minutes). Continue beating, adding enough remaining flour to make dough easy to handle (3 minutes).

3. Stir in all filling ingredients by hand. Turn dough onto lightly floured surface; knead dough until smooth and elastic (about 5 minutes). Shape dough into ball. Place dough in greased bowl; turn greased-side up. Cover; let rise in warm place until double in size (about 1 hour).

4. Punch down dough. Shape into 14 rolls. Place on greased baking sheet. Cover; let rise in warm place until double in size (30 minutes).

5. **Heat oven to 350°.** Combine egg and water in small bowl; brush rolls with egg mixture. Bake for 20 to 25 minutes or until golden brown. *Makes 14 rolls.*

BREAD MACHINE DIRECTIONS: Place all dough ingredients as directed above in bread machine **except use 3¹/2 cups bread flour and reduce water to 1¹/8 cups.** Read instruction manual for your bread machine. Follow directions and use dough setting as directed. Remove dough from bread machine at end of dough cycle. Gently knead in filling ingredients on lightly floured surface. Follow directions above for shaping and raising rolls. Bake for 15 to 20 minutes or until golden brown.

SUBMITTED BY: CHERYL FLYNN, NORTH SIOUX CITY, SD

*"Whenever I bake these rolls for family gatherings,
my niece Bobbi Jo requests an extra batch just for her!"*

BELGIAN-STYLE WAFFLES

Prep: 20 min   Rise: 45 min   Bake: 2 min

Waffles:

1	(¹/4-ounce) package active dry yeast
¹/2	cup warm water (105 to 115°)
2¹/4 cups	LAND O LAKES® Milk
2	cups all-purpose flour
³/4	cup corn flakes
¹/4	cup LAND O LAKES® Butter, melted

3	eggs, beaten
1	tablespoon firmly packed brown sugar
1	teaspoon ground cinnamon
¹/2	teaspoon salt

Toppings:

Strawberries and whipped cream, syrup **or** apple sauce, if desired

1. Dissolve yeast in warm water in large bowl. Add all remaining waffle ingredients; mix well. Let stand in warm place for 45 minutes.

2. Heat waffle iron as directed on manufacturer's instructions. For each waffle, pour **1 cup** batter (amount may vary depending on waffle iron) onto center of hot iron; close top. Bake for 2 to 3 minutes or until steaming stops and waffles are golden brown (timing may vary depending on waffle iron). Repeat with remaining batter.

3. Serve immediately with toppings, if desired. *Makes 6 waffles.*

SUBMITTED BY: SHIRLEY MACIEL, HANFORD, CA

"The secret to the true Belgian waffle is actually the yeast, not the iron.
These waffles are delicious for breakfast and dinner.
The recipe came from my grandmother who was originally from Belgium."

LISA'S BAKING POWDER BISCUIT MUFFINS

Prep: 20 min Bake: 13 min

2½ cups all-purpose flour

¼ cup sugar

4 teaspoons baking powder

¾ cup cold *LAND O LAKES*® Butter

1 cup *LAND O LAKES*® Milk

LAND O LAKES® *Butter, jam* **or** *preserves*

1. Heat oven to 400°. Combine flour, sugar and baking powder in large bowl; cut in butter until crumbly. Stir in milk just until moistened.

2. Spoon batter into two paper-lined or greased 12-cup muffin pans. Bake for 13 to 15 minutes or until lightly browned. Serve hot with butter and jam or preserves. *Makes 2 dozen muffins.*

SUBMITTED BY: LISA A. PIETAN, ELMA, IA

BUTTERSCOTCH BREAD

Prep: 20 min   Bake: 40 min

4 cups all-purpose flour	1½ teaspoons baking powder
2 cups firmly packed brown sugar	1 teaspoon baking soda
2 cups LAND O LAKES® Buttermilk	½ teaspoon salt
2 eggs	1 cup golden raisins **or** chopped nuts
3 tablespoons LAND O LAKES® Butter, melted	

1. Heat oven to 350°. Grease bottoms only of two 9x5-inch loaf pans. Set aside.

2. Combine all ingredients **except** raisins in large mixer bowl. Beat at low speed, scraping bowl often, until well mixed (2 to 3 minutes). Stir in raisins by hand.

3. Spoon batter evenly into prepared loaf pans. Bake for 40 to 50 minutes or until toothpick inserted in center comes out clean. Let stand 10 minutes. Remove from pans. Cool completely. *Makes 2 loaves (24 servings).*

RECIPE TIP: To replace buttermilk, substitute 2 tablespoons vinegar and enough milk to equal 2 cups.

SUBMITTED BY: DOT HARRIS, TOWANDA, PA

"I've been making this bread as long as I've been married--49 years! It's perfect for a buffet or picnic lunch."

SWEETS & DESSERTS

Dessert, the course that's sheer enjoyment!

Fruit Kuchen, page 72

LOUISE'S SUGAR COOKIES

Prep: 30 min   Chill: 1 hr   Bake: 8 min

3	cups all-purpose flour	2	eggs
1/2	teaspoon baking powder	1	cup sugar
1/2	teaspoon baking soda	1	teaspoon vanilla
1/2	teaspoon salt		White **or** decorator sugar for topping
1	cup LAND O LAKES® Butter, softened		

1. Combine flour, baking powder, baking soda and salt in large bowl; cut in butter until crumbly. Set aside.

2. Place eggs in large mixer bowl. Beat at medium-high speed, gradually adding sugar and vanilla, until thick and lemon-colored (1 to 2 minutes). Reduce speed to low; add flour mixture. Beat until well mixed (1 to 2 minutes). Wrap dough in plastic food wrap. Refrigerate until firm (at least 1 hour).

3. **Heat oven to 350°.** Roll out dough on lightly floured surface, one third at a time (keeping remaining dough refrigerated), to 1/4-inch thickness. Cut with assorted scalloped 2 to 2½-inch cookie cutters.

4. Place cookies 1 inch apart on greased cookie sheets. Sprinkle lightly with sugar. Bake for 8 to 10 minutes or until lightly browned. Cool completely. *Makes 4 dozen cookies.*

RECIPE TIP: If desired, omit the sugar topping and frost with powdered sugar icing after baking.

SUBMITTED BY: LOUISE HAINES, BONDURANT, IA

"I am 76 years old and worked in our school kitchen for 21 years. Some people call me the 'Cookie Lady,' because I bake all kinds of cookies. When I make rolled-out sugar cookies, I always use this recipe, because the cookies are tender and keep their shape."

SALTED PEANUT COOKIES

Prep: 45 min   Chill: 2 hrs   Bake: 8 min

3	cups all-purpose flour
2	cups firmly packed brown sugar
1	cup *LAND O LAKES*® Butter, softened
2	eggs
1	teaspoon vanilla
1/2	teaspoon baking soda
1/2	teaspoon cream of tartar
1/8	teaspoon salt
3/4	cup chopped salted peanuts

1. Combine all ingredients **except** peanuts in large mixer bowl. Beat at low speed, scraping bowl often, until well mixed (3 to 4 minutes). Stir in peanuts by hand.

2. Divide dough in thirds. Shape each third into 8-inch roll on lightly floured surface. Wrap rolls in plastic food wrap. Refrigerate at least 2 hours or overnight.

3. **Heat oven to 350°.** Cut rolls into 1/4-inch slices. Place 1 inch apart on ungreased cookie sheets. Bake for 8 to 10 minutes or until lightly browned. *Makes 8 dozen cookies.*

SUBMITTED BY: SYBIL SCHAFER, FLORENCE SD

"This is a recipe my mom made when we were growing up. It remains a favorite with all my sisters."

SUBMITTED BY: CAROLYN MEFFERD, GILMORE CITY, IA

"This recipe is from my father's mother, who came from Denmark. She and her husband raised 17 children, including two sets of twins. My father, who is 86 years old, tells me that whatever his mother made— it always went."

GRANDMA'S SOUR CREAM COOKIES

Prep: 40 min   Bake: 10 min

1	cup firmly packed brown sugar
1/2	cup LAND O LAKES® Butter, softened
1/2	cup LAND O LAKES® Sour Cream
1	egg
1	teaspoon vanilla
2 1/2	cups all-purpose flour
1	teaspoon baking soda
1/2	cup chopped dates **or** raisins
1/2	cup chopped nuts

1. Heat oven to 350°. Combine brown sugar and butter in large mixer bowl. Beat at medium speed, scraping bowl often, until creamy (1 to 2 minutes). Add sour cream, egg and vanilla. Continue beating until well mixed (1 to 2 minutes). Reduce speed to low; add flour and baking soda. Beat until well mixed (1 to 2 minutes). Stir in dates and nuts by hand.

2. Drop dough by rounded teaspoonfuls 2 inches apart onto ungreased cookie sheets. Bake for 10 to 12 minutes or until set and golden brown. *Makes 4 dozen cookies.*

LITTLE PIGGY COOKIES

Prep: 1 hr   Bake: 10 min   Cool: 15 min

Cookies:

1½ cups sugar

1   cup *LAND O LAKES® Butter, melted*

2   eggs

1   teaspoon vanilla

3½ cups all-purpose flour

1   teaspoon baking soda

½   teaspoon salt

Frosting:

2   cups powdered sugar

¼   cup *LAND O LAKES® Butter, softened*

1   teaspoon vanilla

2 to 3 tablespoons *LAND O LAKES® Milk*

Decorations:

Pink sugar wafer cookies

12   marshmallows

Red food color

Plain candy-coated chocolate pieces

1. Heat oven to 350°. Combine sugar, 1 cup melted butter, eggs and vanilla in large mixer bowl. Beat at medium speed, scraping bowl often, until well mixed (1 to 2 minutes). Reduce speed to low; add flour, baking soda and salt. Beat until well mixed (1 to 2 minutes).

2. Drop dough by rounded teaspoonfuls onto lightly greased cookie sheets. Flatten dough with bottom of glass. Bake for 10 to 12 minutes or until golden brown. Cool completely.

3. Combine powdered sugar, ¼ cup butter and vanilla in small mixer bowl. Beat at low speed, scraping bowl often and gradually adding enough milk for desired spreading consistency. Frost cooled cookies.

4. For ears, cut sugar wafer cookies into triangles. Place two triangles in top of frosted cookie. For snout, cut marshmallows in half crosswise; place **one-half** in center of bottom half of each cookie. Use point of toothpick dipped in red food color to mark nostrils. For eyes, use color-matched candy pieces. *Makes 2 dozen cookies.*

"It's so fun to watch kid's faces light up when presented with these edible pig faces. I got this recipe from my mother-in-law who saw them at a Christmas cookie exchange. They were a hit there, and still are a hit wherever I take them."

FRUIT KUCHEN

Prep: 30 min   Bake: 50 min

Cake:

1   cup sugar

2   eggs

1   cup LAND O LAKES® Sour Cream

2   cups all-purpose flour

2   teaspoons baking powder

1   teaspoon salt

1/2   teaspoon baking soda

Topping:

1 to 1 1/2 pounds fresh fruit (pitted cherries, sliced peaches, blueberries, raspberries **and/or** prune plums, seeded, halved)

1   cup sugar

1   cup LAND O LAKES® Sour Cream
     LAND O LAKES® Half-and-Half, if desired

1. Heat oven to 350°. Spray 13x9-inch baking pan with no stick cooking spray. Set aside.

2. Combine 1 cup sugar and eggs in medium mixer bowl. Beat at medium speed, scraping bowl often, until light and lemon-colored (1 to 2 minutes). Stir in 1 cup sour cream. Reduce speed to low; add flour, baking powder, salt and baking soda. Beat until well mixed (1 to 2 minutes).

3. Pour batter into prepared pan. Arrange fruit evenly over batter. (If using plums, arrange halves, skin-side up.) Sprinkle 1 cup sugar over fruit; spread with 1 cup sour cream. Bake for 50 to 60 minutes or until golden brown.

4. Serve warm with half-and-half, if desired. *Makes 12 servings.*

RECIPE TIP: Reduce the oven temperature to 325° if you are using a 13x9-inch glass baking dish.

SUBMITTED BY: KAY ALLAN, YAKIMA, WA

CRANBERRY TARTS

Prep: 1 hr   Bake: 22 min

1   cup all-purpose flour

1/2   cup *LAND O LAKES*® Butter, softened

1   (3-ounce) package cream cheese, softened

3/4   cup sugar

1/2   cup chopped pecans

1   egg

2   tablespoons *LAND O LAKES*® Butter

1   teaspoon vanilla

48 to 72 fresh cranberries, washed, drained

1. Heat oven to 325°. Combine flour, 1/2 cup butter and cream cheese in small mixer bowl. Beat at medium speed until dough forms a ball (1 to 2 minutes). Divide dough into 24 equal pieces. Place **1 piece** in each mini muffin pan cup; press evenly on bottom and up sides.

2. Combine sugar, pecans, egg, 2 tablespoons butter and vanilla in small bowl. Place **2 or 3** cranberries in each pastry-lined cup. Spoon **2 teaspoonfuls** sugar mixture over cranberries.

3. Bake for 22 to 25 minutes or until golden brown. Loosen tarts from pan while hot by running knife around inside of rim. Cool completely; remove from pans. *Makes 24 tarts.*

SHOOFLY PIE

Prep: 30 min   Bake: 55 min

Crust:

1   cup all-purpose flour

$^1/_8$ teaspoon salt

$^1/_3$ cup cold LAND O LAKES® Butter

3 to 4 tablespoons cold water

Filling:

$^3/_4$ cup boiling water

$^3/_4$ teaspoon baking soda

1   cup dark **or** light molasses (not unsulfered)

1$^3/_4$ cups all-purpose flour

$^3/_4$ cup firmly packed brown sugar

$^1/_8$ teaspoon baking soda

$^1/_8$ teaspoon cream of tartar

$^1/_2$ cup cold LAND O LAKES® Butter

1   egg, beaten

1   tablespoon firmly packed brown sugar

1   tablespoon sugar

1. Combine 1 cup flour and salt in medium bowl; cut in $^1/_3$ cup butter until crumbly. Mix in water with fork until flour is moistened. Shape into a ball. Roll dough into 12-inch circle on lightly floured surface. Place in 10-inch pie plate. Crimp or flute crust.

2. Combine boiling water and $^3/_4$ teaspoon baking soda in medium bowl. Stir in molasses. Set aside to cool.

3. Combine 1$^3/_4$ cups flour, $^3/_4$ cup brown sugar, $^1/_8$ teaspoon baking soda and cream of tartar in another medium bowl; cut in $^1/_2$ cup butter until mixture resembles coarse crumbs. Set aside.

4. **Heat oven to 400°.** Add egg, 1 tablespoon brown sugar and 1 tablespoon sugar to molasses mixture; mix well. Stir **half** of flour mixture into molasses mixture. Pour into prepared crust; sprinkle with remaining flour mixture.

5. Bake for 10 minutes. **Reduce oven temperature to 350°.** Continue baking for 45 to 50 minutes or until filling is set. Serve warm. *Makes 12 servings.*

RECIPE TIP: Substitute 9$^1/_2$-inch (24cm) deep dish pie plate for 10-inch pie plate. Bake as directed above. *10 servings.*

SUBMITTED BY: MRS. VERNA MAE LAPP, LANCASTER, PA

SUGAR-CRUSTED APPLE PIE

Prep: 45 min   Chill: 1 hr   Bake: 55 min

Crust:

4	cups all-purpose flour
1	teaspoon salt
1	cup cold LAND O LAKES® Butter
1	cup shortening
½	cup cold water

1	egg, beaten
1	teaspoon apple cider vinegar **or** white vinegar

Filling:

12	cups (4 pounds) tart cooking apples, peeled, cored, sliced ¼-inch

2¼	cups sugar
2	tablespoons all-purpose flour
3	teaspoons ground cinnamon
6	tablespoons LAND O LAKES® Butter, cut into pieces

1. Combine 4 cups flour and salt in large bowl; cut in 1 cup butter and shortening until crumbly.

2. Combine cold water, egg and vinegar in small bowl. Add egg mixture to flour mixture; mix with fork until flour is just moistened. Divide pastry into fourths; shape each fourth into a ball. Wrap each in plastic food wrap; refrigerate at least 1 hour.

3. Roll one pastry ball into 12-inch circle on lightly floured surface. Place in 9-inch pie plate. Trim pastry to ½ inch from rim of pan. Set aside.

4. **Heat oven to 350°.** Combine **6 cups** apples, **1 cup** sugar, **1 tablespoon** flour and **1½ teaspoons** cinnamon in large bowl; toss to coat. Spoon apple mixture into prepared crust. Dot apple mixture with **3 tablespoons** butter.

5. Roll second pastry ball into 12-inch circle; cut 8 large slits in top crust. Place over pie; seal, trim and crimp or flute edge. Sprinkle top of crust evenly with 2 tablespoons sugar.

6. Cover edge of crust with 2-inch strip of aluminum foil. Bake for 45 minutes; remove aluminum foil. Continue baking for 10 to 20 minutes or until crust is lightly browned and juice begins to bubble through slits in crust. Let pie stand 20 to 30 minutes before cutting.

7. While first pie bakes, repeat rolling and filling process to make a second pie. Seal in resealable plastic freezer bag. Freeze for up to 3 months. To bake, thaw frozen pie while oven preheats, then bake as directed above. *Makes 2 pies (8 servings each).*

*There were 15 kids in our family and when it was apple pie-baking time,
we girls would form an assembly line to peel, slice and fill the pies.
But doing the crusts was always reserved for mom. After packing our freezer full,
we loaded the car to deliver pies to our neighbors. This tradition of sharing pies
has now been passed down to my children."*

WISCONSIN SOUR CREAM RAISIN PIE

Prep: 25 min   Cook: 15 min   Bake: 10 min

Pie:

1	9-inch single baked pie pastry
1	cup raisins
1	cup boiling water
1	cup sugar
6	tablespoons all-purpose flour
1/8	teaspoon salt

2 1/4	cups LAND O LAKES® Milk
3	egg yolks
1/2	cup LAND O LAKES® Sour Cream
1/4	cup LAND O LAKES® Butter

Meringue:

1/2	cup hot water
1	tablespoon cornstarch

3	egg whites, room temperature
1/8	teaspoon cream of tartar
1/8	teaspoon salt
6	tablespoons sugar
1/2	teaspoon vanilla

1. Place pastry in 9-inch pie plate. Crimp or flute crust. Set aside.

2. Place raisins in small bowl. Cover with boiling water; let stand 5 minutes to plump raisins. Drain.

3. Combine 1 cup sugar, flour and 1/8 teaspoon salt in 4-quart saucepan. Gradually stir in milk. Cook over medium heat, stirring constantly, until bubbly and thickened (7 to 9 minutes). Remove from heat.

4. Place egg yolks in small bowl; mix well. Gradually stir **1 cup** milk mixture into beaten yolks. Return egg mixture to saucepan, stirring constantly. Cook over medium heat, stirring constantly, until mixture is thickened and coats back of metal spoon (3 to 5 minutes). Continue cooking, stirring constantly, 2 minutes. Remove from heat. Stir in drained raisins, sour cream and butter. DO NOT OVER-MIX.

5. Combine hot water and cornstarch in 1-quart saucepan. Cook over medium heat, stirring constantly, until mixture comes to a boil and is clear and thickened (3 to 4 minutes). Cover; place in refrigerator to cool slightly (8 to 10 minutes).

6. **Heat oven to 350°.** Meanwhile, combine egg whites, cream of tartar and 1/8 teaspoon salt in large mixer bowl. Beat at high speed until foamy (1 to 2 minutes). Continue beating, gradually adding 6 tablespoons sugar until glossy and soft peaks form (5 to 6 minutes). Add cornstarch mixture and vanilla to egg white mixture; beat until smooth (1 to 2 minutes).

7. Pour hot raisin filling into prepared pastry. Spread meringue over hot raisin filling, sealing to edges. Bake for 10 to 12 minutes or until meringue is golden brown. Cool on wire rack before serving. Cover; store refrigerated. *Makes 8 servings.*

FROZEN PUMPKIN SQUARES

Prep: 20 min   Bake: 8 min   Freeze: 8 hrs

Crust:

1³/4 cups (about 24) graham cracker crumbs

¹/2 cup powdered sugar

¹/2 cup chopped nuts

¹/2 cup LAND O LAKES® Butter, melted

Filling:

1 cup sugar

1 (15-ounce) can pumpkin

1 teaspoon ground cinnamon

1 teaspoon ground cloves

1 teaspoon ground ginger

¹/2 gallon LAND O LAKES® Vanilla Ice Cream, softened

LAND O LAKES® Whipping Cream, whipped, if desired

Chopped nuts, if desired

1. Heat oven to 350°. Stir together all crust ingredients in medium bowl. Press evenly onto bottom of ungreased 13x9-inch baking pan. Bake for 8 minutes or until lightly browned. Cool completely.

2. Meanwhile, combine sugar, pumpkin, cinnamon, cloves and ginger in large bowl; mix well. Add ice cream; stir to combine.

3. Spread ice cream mixture over baked crust. Cover; freeze 8 hours or overnight.

4. To serve, cut into squares. Garnish with whipped cream or chopped nuts, if desired. Store in freezer. *Makes 18 servings.*

RECIPE TIP: This dessert can be made ahead and frozen for up to two weeks.

SUBMITTED BY: DOREEN FRERICKS, MELROSE, MN

"My husband likes this recipe because it's different from a traditional pumpkin pie. Sometimes I make it using home-grown pumpkin!"

FRUIT PUDDING DESSERT

Prep: 20 min

1   cup *LAND O LAKES*® Sour Cream
1   cup *LAND O LAKES*® Milk
1/4 cup frozen orange juice concentrate, thawed
1   (3-ounce) package vanilla instant pudding and pie filling
1   (20-ounce) can pineapple chunks, drained
1   (11-ounce) can mandarin orange segments, drained
2   medium tart red apples, cored, chopped
1   banana, sliced

1. Combine sour cream, milk, orange juice concentrate and instant pudding in large serving bowl; mix until smooth.

2. Add fruit; mix lightly to coat. *Makes 12 servings (2/3 cup each).*

SUBMITTED BY: WANDA L. YODER, BELLEVILLE, PA

CARAMEL APPLE NOODLE KUGEL

Prep: 45 min   Bake: 50 min

Kugel:

6   cups (12 ounces) uncooked dried egg noodles

1   cup LAND O LAKES® Milk

1/4   cup LAND O LAKES® Butter

2   (8-ounce) packages cream cheese, cubed

1/2   cup sugar

1   tablespoon vegetable oil

1   teaspoon grated lemon peel

1   teaspoon grated orange peel

2   teaspoons lemon juice

1/2   teaspoon vanilla

1/4   teaspoon ground nutmeg

4   eggs

Topping:

3   large (5 cups) tart green cooking apples, cored, peeled, chopped

3   tablespoons sugar

1   teaspoon ground cinnamon

1   cup crushed corn flakes (3 cups whole flakes)

1/4   cup LAND O LAKES® Butter, melted

3   tablespoons firmly packed brown sugar

1   cup caramel apple dip **or** ice cream topping, warmed

1. Cook noodles according to package directions. Drain.

2. **Heat oven to 350°.** Combine milk, 1/4 cup butter and cream cheese in medium saucepan. Cook over low heat, stirring occasionally, until smooth (5 to 7 minutes). Remove from heat.

3. Combine 1/2 cup sugar, oil, lemon peel, orange peel, lemon juice, vanilla and nutmeg in large bowl; mix well. Add eggs; mix well. Add cream cheese mixture; mix well. Stir in cooked noodles.

4. Spoon into greased 13x9-inch pan. Combine apples, 3 tablespoons sugar and cinnamon in medium bowl. Spoon apple mixture over noodle mixture; gently pat apples into noodles.

5. Combine corn flakes, 1/4 cup melted butter and brown sugar in small bowl; sprinkle over apples. Bake for 50 to 60 minutes or until knife inserted in center comes out clean.

6. To serve, cut into pieces. Serve warm drizzled with caramel apple dip. *Makes 15 servings.*

SUBMITTED BY: PAULA J. ROETH, MARYSVILLE, OH

NONNY'S FRUITCAKE

Prep: 1 hr   Bake: 45 min   Cool: 1 hr

Fruitcake:

1   cup chunky-style applesauce

2   teaspoons baking soda

4   cups all-purpose flour

2   cups walnuts **or** pecans, coarsely chopped

1½ cups chopped dates

1   cup currants

1   cup dark raisins

1   cup golden raisins

2   teaspoons ground cinnamon

1   teaspoon ground nutmeg

½   teaspoon salt

½   teaspoon ground cloves

1   (8-ounce) can crushed pineapple, undrained

1   (6-ounce) jar maraschino cherries, coarsely chopped, **reserve liquid**

1   cup LAND O LAKES® Butter, softened

2   cups firmly packed brown sugar

2   eggs

½   cup whiskey

Glaze:

2   tablespoons firmly packed brown sugar

2   tablespoons water

1   tablespoon light corn syrup

2   teaspoons lemon juice

     Candied red and green cherries, if desired

     Walnut **or** pecan halves, if desired

1. Heat oven to 325°. Combine applesauce and baking soda in small bowl; mix well. Set aside.

2. Combine flour, walnuts, dates, currants, raisins, cinnamon, nutmeg, salt and cloves in large bowl. Add applesauce mixture, pineapple, cherries and reserved cherry liquid; mix well.

3. Combine butter, brown sugar and eggs in very large mixer bowl. Beat at medium speed, scraping bowl often, until creamy (1 to 2 minutes). Add fruit mixture; continue beating until well mixed (1 to 2 minutes).

4. Spoon batter into 8 greased (5x3-inch) mini loaf pans. Bake for 45 to 50 minutes or until toothpick inserted in center comes out clean. Remove cakes from oven. Place on wire racks; let stand 10 minutes. Remove cakes from pans, if desired. While cakes are still warm, drizzle each cake with **1 tablespoon** whiskey. Cool completely.

5. Combine all glaze ingredients **except** cherries and walnuts in 1-quart saucepan. Cook over medium heat, stirring occasionally, until clear and slightly thickened (3 to 5 minutes). Decorate with cherries and nuts, if desired. Spoon glaze over cooled fruitcakes. Wrap cakes in plastic food wrap, then in foil. Store in cool place or refrigerate. *Makes 8 mini cakes (8 slices per cake).*

RECIPE TIP: You may substitute ½ cup orange or apple juice for the whiskey in this recipe.

SUBMITTED BY: PATRICIA MILLER, MINNEAPOLIS, MN

"I've won over numerous fruitcake converts with my grandmother's rich, dark version of this holiday tradition. Nonny made it in November so that it would mellow by Christmas, and my mother did the same. I make it every year, too, and love serving it on cookie trays."

85
SWEETS & DESSERTS

GINA'S SCRUMPTIOUS CHEESECAKE

Prep: 20 min   Bake: 55 min   Chill: 3 hrs

Crust:

1   cup graham cracker crumbs

2   tablespoons sugar

2   tablespoons *LAND O LAKES*® *Butter, melted*

Filling:

1½ cups sugar

4   (8-ounce) packages cream cheese, softened

2   teaspoons vanilla

4   eggs

Topping:

1½ cups *LAND O LAKES*® *Sour Cream*

¼   cup sugar

2   teaspoons vanilla

     Fresh fruit, if desired

1. Heat oven to 350°. Stir together all crust ingredients in small bowl. Press evenly onto bottom of 9x3-inch springform pan.

2. Combine 1½ cups sugar, cream cheese and 2 teaspoons vanilla in large mixer bowl. Beat at medium speed, scraping bowl often, until creamy (3 to 4 minutes). Add eggs, one at a time, beating well after each addition (1 to 2 minutes).

3. Pour batter into prepared pan. Bake for 55 to 65 minutes or until center is set two inches from edge of pan.

4. Combine all topping ingredients in small bowl. Spread over cheesecake. Continue baking for 10 minutes. Loosen sides of cheesecake from rim of pan by running knife around inside of pan. Cool completely.

5. Loosely cover; refrigerate at least 3 hours before serving. Top with fresh fruit, if desired. *Makes 16 servings.*

SUBMITTED BY: GINA GIACOMAZZI, HANFORD, CA

"I get many requests to bring this cheesecake to dinners with friends and family.
My favorite way to serve it is topped with fresh red raspberries and shaved chocolate.
For the fourth of July I decorate it with raspberries and blueberries.
Once on St. Patrick's day I stenciled a shamrock on top using green sugar!"

MARIE'S CHOCOLATE CAKE

Prep: 15 min   Bake: 40 min

2   cups sugar

1/2   cup *LAND O LAKES® Butter, softened*

1/2   cup sour milk

2   *(1-ounce) squares unsweetened chocolate,*
        melted

2   eggs

2   *teaspoons vanilla*

2   *cups all-purpose flour*

2   *teaspoons baking soda*

1/2   *teaspoon salt*

1   *cup boiling water*

        *Powdered sugar **or** whipped cream, if desired*

1. Heat oven to 350°. Combine sugar and butter in large mixer bowl. Beat at medium speed until creamy (1 to 2 minutes). Add milk, melted chocolate, eggs and vanilla. Continue beating until smooth (1 to 2 minutes). Reduce speed to low; add flour, baking soda and salt. Beat until well mixed (2 to 3 minutes). Add boiling water; continue beating until smooth (1 to 2 minutes).

2. Pour batter into greased and floured 13x9-inch baking pan. Bake for 40 to 45 minutes or until toothpick inserted in center comes out clean. Dust cake with powdered sugar or serve with dollop of whipped cream, if desired. *Makes 15 servings.*

RECIPE TIP: To make 1/2 cup sour milk, add 1 1/2 teaspoons vinegar plus enough milk to equal 1/2 cup.

SUBMITTED BY: BRUCE KIRKING, BROOKLYN PARK, MN

"Growing up, we always ate this chocolate cake. It is a recipe from the mother of a young lady, Marie, whom my uncle was courting at the time. Before getting married, WWII broke out. My uncle did not want to leave a widow behind in case he didn't return—so they waited. Sadly, my uncle was killed in service. After that, Marie never married. Recently, on my grandmother's 90th birthday, a woman by the name of Marie came to visit her. I finally got to meet Marie, the namesake of the best chocolate cake and my would-be aunt."

SUBMITTED BY: DIANE FRANZEEN, ARLINGTON, MN

"This recipe was one of my grandma's favorites. Every time there was a birthday or a family reunion, our whole family would request that grandma would bake this special cake. It tastes like angel food cake and just melts in your mouth."

OVERNIGHT CAKE

Prep: 40 min   Stand: 8 hrs   Bake: 30 min   Cool: 1 hr

Cake:

2	cups cake flour
2	cups sugar
1	cup boiling water
1	tablespoon baking powder
1½	teaspoons almond extract
1	teaspoon vanilla
6	egg whites, room temperature
1	teaspoon cream of tartar
½	teaspoon salt

Topping:

1	cup LAND O LAKES® Sour Cream
6	egg yolks
1	cup sugar
	Pinch salt
1	teaspoon grated lemon rind
1	teaspoon vanilla
	Toasted coconut **or** finely chopped nuts, if desired

1. Combine cake flour and sugar in large bowl. Add boiling water; mix well. Cover; let stand at room temperature or refrigerate 8 hours or overnight.

2. **Heat oven to 350°.** Add baking powder, almond extract and vanilla to flour mixture; mix well. Set aside.

3. Combine egg whites, cream of tartar and salt in large mixer bowl. Beat at medium speed until glossy and stiff peaks form (3 to 5 minutes). Gently stir egg whites into flour mixture. Spoon batter into ungreased 13x9-inch baking pan. Bake for 30 to 35 minutes or until toothpick inserted in center comes out clean.

4. Invert baking pan on cooling rack. Cool completely before removing from pan. Loosen sides of cake from rim of pan by running knife around inside of pan. Place cake on serving platter.

5. Meanwhile, combine all topping ingredients **except** coconut in 2-quart heavy saucepan. Cook over low heat, stirring constantly, until thickened and mixture reaches 160°F (15 to 20 minutes). Cool completely (30 minutes).

6. Spread top and sides of cooled cake with topping. Sprinkle with coconut or nuts, if desired. *Makes 15 servings.*

RECIPE TIP: You may substitute 2 cups all-purpose flour minus ¼ cup for the cake flour in this recipe.

DAIRY COUNTRY
CHOCOLATE SHEET CAKE

Prep: 30 min   Bake: 20 min

Cake:

1	cup *LAND O LAKES® Butter*
1	cup *water*
1/4	cup *unsweetened cocoa*
2	cups *all-purpose flour*
2	cups *sugar*
1/2	teaspoon *salt*
1/2	cup *LAND O LAKES® Light Sour Cream*
2	*eggs*
1	teaspoon *baking soda*

Frosting:

1/2	cup *LAND O LAKES® Butter*
1/4	cup *unsweetened cocoa*
6	tablespoons *LAND O LAKES® Milk*
3 1/2	cups (1 pound) *powdered sugar*
1	cup *chopped nuts*
1	teaspoon *vanilla*

1. Heat oven to 350°. Combine 1 cup butter, water and 1/4 cup cocoa in 3-quart saucepan. Cook over medium heat, stirring occasionally, until mixture comes to a boil (6 to 7 minutes). Remove pan from heat. Add flour, sugar and salt; mix well. Add sour cream, eggs and baking soda; beat until smooth.

2. Spread batter into greased 15x10x1-inch jelly roll pan. Bake for 20 to 22 minutes or until toothpick inserted in center comes out clean.

3. Meanwhile, combine 1/2 cup butter, 1/4 cup cocoa and milk in 2-quart saucepan. Cook over medium heat, stirring occasionally, until mixture comes to a boil (3 to 4 minutes).

4. Remove from heat. Add powdered sugar; beat until fluffy. Stir in nuts and vanilla. Spread over warm cake. *Makes 60 servings.*

INDEX